# M·O·V·I·E

# MONSTERS

# M·O·V·I·E
# MONSTERS

## by Tom Powers

Lerner Publications Company
Minneapolis

## Acknowledgments

The photographs in this book are reproduced through the courtesy of: pp. 1, 31, 33, 34, 42, 48, 51, 55, 58, 63, 68, 69, 73, 74, 76, Photofest; pp. 2, 11, 16, 24, 27, 29, 41, 43, 44, 49, 53, 59, 62, 64, 65, Hollywood Book and Poster Co.; pp. 6, 10, 13, 18, 19, 20, 21, 23, 25, 30, 39, 47, 66, 78, Wisconsin Center for Film and Theater Research; pp. 8, 37, 38, 52, 60, 70, 77, Museum of Modern Art/Film Stills Archive.

Front cover photograph by Photofest. Back cover photograph courtesy of Wisconsin Center for Film and Theater Research.

*This edition of this book is available in two bindings:*
Library binding by Lerner Publications Company
Soft cover by First Avenue Editions
241 First Avenue North
Minneapolis, Minnesota 55401

LIBRARY OF CONGRESS CATALOGING-IN-PUBLICATION DATA

Powers, Tom (Tom J.)
    Movie monsters / by Tom Powers.
        p.   cm.
    Bibliography: p.
    Includes index.
    Summary: Describes the great monsters of the movies and the films in which they appeared. Includes King Kong, Godzilla, Frankenstein, the Thing, Wolf Man, and the Gremlins.
    ISBN 0-8225-1637-3 (lib. bdg.)
    ISBN 0-8225-9571-0 (pbk.)
    1. Monsters in motion pictures—Juvenile literature.  2. Horror films—History and criticism—Juvenile literature.  3. Science fiction films—History and criticism—Juvenile literature.
    [1. Monsters in motion pictures.  2. Horror films—History and criticism.  3. Science fiction films—History and criticism.]
    I. Title.
PN1995.9M6P69   1989                                            88-35982
791.43'09'9916-dc19
                                                                      CIP
                                                                      AC

Manufactured in the United States of America

2   3   4   5   6   7   8   9   10   99   98   97   96   95   94   93   92   91   90

# Contents

# INTRODUCTION

We all have a monster inside us. That monster is fear. Fear can prevent us from living our lives fully, from doing the things we really want to do.

Some people are afraid of heights, and others fear water. Some people dread losing control, while others are afraid of being laughed at. Most people fear death or pain. A little bit of fear is not a bad thing. It is one of the feelings that makes us human. When fear grows too strong inside us, however, we run the risk that it will take over our lives. Fear that has been bottled up for too long can break out and grip us like a giant monster.

Monster movies provide us with a safe and easy way to let out our fears. Sitting alone in the dark, we wonder where the Thing or the Gremlins will pop up next. Sometimes we want to scream as the tension mounts, but we hold it back, waiting until we can't stand it any longer. Then we scream with fear and delight. This is the pleasure that a scary monster movie gives us.

Audiences cheered for King Kong in 1933.

Most movie monsters frighten us, but some monsters also invite our sympathy. The Wolf Man is not only scary, he is lonely and different and tormented by a body that has gone out of control. Frankenstein's monster may be a murderer, but he is also innocent and childlike. We feel sorry for these characters even while they scare us.

Some movie monsters, like King Kong and Godzilla, appeal to the hidden fears of whole nations. During the 1930s, people in the United States felt trapped by the Great Depression, which left millions of people hungry and out of work. When movie audiences watched King Kong in chains, they thought of the strength of their nation, which was suffering from circumstances it could not control. When Kong broke free, audiences cheered.

Godzilla evoked similar feelings in Japanese people during the 1950s. The monster at first seemed to stand for the horror of the atomic bombs that had been dropped on two Japanese cities in 1945. Audiences were delighted to see the monster defeated and peace restored. In later movies, though, Godzilla became Japan's protector; he began to represent the hidden strength of the Japanese people.

Some movie monsters have become permanent parts of a nation's culture. King Kong first appeared in the 1930s. A smaller movie ape named *Mighty Joe Young* was popular with audiences in the 1940s. Kong later starred in a remake of his original story in the 1970s. The Wolf Man, who first appeared in a 1941 film, has recently popped up in movies like *An American Werewolf in London* (1981) and *Teen Wolf* (1985). The story of Frankenstein's monster has been retold in *Young Frankenstein* (1974) and *The Bride* (1985). Godzilla has appeared in more than a dozen Japanese movies.

Why do certain movie monsters continue to fascinate us? The answer seems to lie in the monsters' human qualities. These creatures represent basic human fears that never go away. They show us what our own lives might be like if our fears came true.

Note: The following abbreviations are used in this book:
*b/w* black and white
*dir* director
*pro* producer
*st* starring
*sp eff* special effects

(1931)

# FRANKENSTEIN

*b/w*
*dir* James Whale
*pro* Carl Laemmle, Jr.
*st* Boris Karloff, Colin Clive, Mae
  Clark
*makeup* Jack Pierce

"Frankenstein" is the name of a mad scientist who creates a monster that terrorizes the German countryside in the early 1800s. Over the years, many people have come to associate the name "Frankenstein" with the monster itself. In fact, the creature has no name. Unlike most Japanese monsters, who have specific names (such as Godzilla, Ghidrah, Rodan, and Mothra), American movie monsters usually have only vague, general labels: the Thing, the Creature, the Alien, the Blob, Them, the Wolf Man, and so forth. But one American monster who does have a name is King Kong. Another is the monster shark in *Jaws* (his name is Bruce). Frankenstein's monster is called simply "the Monster."

## "You Have Created a Monster and It Will Destroy You"

As the film *Frankenstein* begins, a coffin is being lowered into a grave. Beneath a gloomy sky, the friends and family of the dead man weep and wail.

Two men watch this scene from behind the cemetery fence. After the funeral party has left, young Henry Frankenstein and his assistant Fritz sneak into the graveyard and dig up the dead man's coffin. Frankenstein pats the coffin. He tells Fritz that the dead man is not really dead—"just resting, waiting for a new life to come."

Frankenstein sends Fritz to steal a brain from a nearby medical school. Fritz is a strange, hunchbacked man, fearful, cruel, and not too smart. Inside the medical school, he finds two brains on display in jars. One of the brains is normal. The other is the brain of a vicious criminal.

Fritz picks up the jar containing the normal brain and begins to rush out of the room when he is startled by a loud noise. He drops the jar, and it smashes on the floor. Fritz grabs the other jar and hurries away.

The next night, a violent storm rages outside the old stone tower where Frankenstein keeps his laboratory. Inside, Frankenstein prepares to conduct his final experiment. Using parts of different bodies and the brain that Fritz stole from the medical school, Frankenstein has put together a large, lifeless creature. He has designed a whole network of electrical wires and switches to harness the power of lightning bolts, which, he is convinced, will bring the creature to life.

Suddenly there is a loud knocking at the tower's heavy wooden door. Frankenstein's fiancee, Elizabeth, his friend Victor, and his university professor Dr. Waldman have come to stop his experiment.

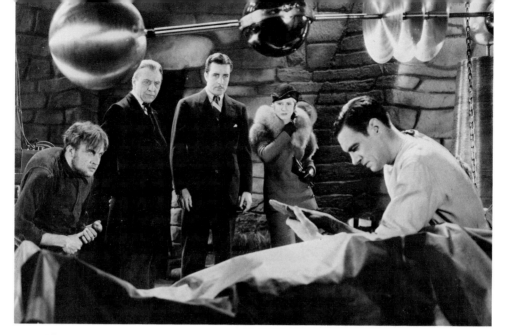

Henry Frankenstein works to bring his creature to life.

At first Frankenstein does not want his visitors to know what he is doing, but Victor angers him by calling him "crazy." Frankenstein does look crazy. His face is thin and pale, his eyes flash with anger, and his thick black hair tumbles over his forehead.

Determined to show his guests that he is not crazy, Frankenstein invites them to come up into the tower. The experiment is about to begin.

With Fritz's help, Frankenstein raises the lifeless body on a platform that moves up to an opening at the top of the tower. Lightning flashes, and electric arcs jump from machine to machine. Frankenstein's friends watch in horror. Finally, the platform is lowered back into the laboratory.

At first, nothing seems to have happened. Then one of the creature's hands, sticking out from under a sheet, slowly begins to move. "It's alive!" Frankenstein shouts. "It's alive!"

The next day, Victor and Elizabeth talk to Baron Frankenstein, Henry's father. The Baron decides to visit his son and bring him home. Meanwhile, Dr. Waldman has remained at the tower. The professor tells Frankenstein that he has mistakenly implanted a criminal brain in his creature. "Only evil can come of it," Dr. Waldman says. "You have created a monster and it will destroy you."

As they talk, Frankenstein's monster lurches into the room. He looks like a giant man—perhaps seven feet tall. He wears a dark suit and thick, heavy boots. His coat sleeves are much too short for his long arms.

The monster's face is truly frightening. A jagged scar runs down his forehead, and another scar shows where his head was sliced open to have a brain implanted. The monster's forehead is much larger than a normal man's, and dark circles ring his eyes. The bolts that acted as electrical connectors stick out from the sides of the creature's neck.

Frankenstein tells the monster to sit down in a chair. Slowly, he does so. "You see," Frankenstein tells Dr. Waldman, "it understands." Frankenstein opens a curtain, and the monster sees sunlight for the first time. The creature smiles and reaches for the light, trying to grab it in his huge, scarred hands. When Fritz enters with a lighted torch, however, the monster panics and becomes violent. The three men have to wrestle the monster to the floor. They then carry him downstairs and chain him in the cellar of the old tower.

In the cellar, cruel Fritz delights in whipping the creature and teasing it with a flaming torch. But he teases the monster one time too many. Up in the laboratory, Frankenstein and Dr. Waldman hear terrible screams. By the time they reach the cellar, the monster has murdered Fritz. The monster turns on Frankenstein and Dr. Waldman, but the two men knock him unconscious with a strong drug.

Henry Frankenstein has grown more and more unhappy with the result of his experiment. He seems not to know what to do next. When his father and Elizabeth arrive at the tower, he allows them to take him home.

Dr. Waldman stays behind to kill the giant creature. The monster, however, awakens and strangles the doctor. Then slowly, with giant, powerful steps, he leaves the tower and walks into the countryside.

Near a lake, the monster meets a little girl named Maria. Innocently, Maria invites the creature to play with her. She throws flowers in the lake and shows him how they float on the surface of the water. The monster playfully reaches for Maria and throws her in the lake, too.

Meanwhile, the Frankenstein family is preparing to celebrate the marriage of Henry and Elizabeth. All the people of their village are playing music and dancing in the streets. But Elizabeth is worried and afraid. She wonders why Dr. Waldman has not arrived for the wedding. She tells Henry, "Something is coming between us."

Elizabeth is right. News arrives that Dr. Waldman has been murdered. Then the monster creeps into Elizabeth's bedroom and nearly kills her. The celebration in the village comes to a sudden halt when Maria's father walks down the main street, carrying the body of his drowned daughter.

The villagers grab torches and pitchforks and form search parties to find the murdering creature. Henry Frankenstein leads one group into the mountains, where he becomes separated from the other villagers. Wandering alone, Frankenstein finds himself face to face with the monster he created. The monster beats and chokes Frankenstein, then carries him off to an old, abandoned windmill.

After innocently tossing flowers into the lake with Maria, the monster throws the little girl in, too. Enraged over her death, the villagers form a search party to find and kill Frankenstein's creature.

As the villagers surround the windmill, the monster snarls at them. He throws Frankenstein out of a high window. The scientist hits one of the windmill blades, then tumbles to the ground. He is badly hurt, but still alive.

The villagers light the windmill on fire. Inside, the monster waves his arms and runs around in a panic, tormented by fire one last time. As the windmill goes up in flames around the monster, the villagers carry Frankenstein home. There, Elizabeth will nurse him back to health and help him forget his mad dream of creating human life.

## A SYMPATHETIC MONSTER

The story of *Frankenstein* was written by an 18-year-old girl, Mary Wollstonecraft Shelley, in 1816. Mary Shelley was not an ordinary young woman. Mary's mother had been a writer, which was not common in those days, and her husband was the great poet Percy Bysshe Shelley. For 30 years after his death, Mary Shelley kept her husband's heart, wrapped in a piece of linen.

No one in 19th-century Europe had ever encountered a story quite so strange and terrifying as Mary Shelley's *Frankenstein*. It was turned into a popular play, and during the era of the silent movies, it was filmed three times. The first sound version of *Frankenstein*, however, is the movie everyone remembers.

Much of the success of the movie *Frankenstein* is due to Boris Karloff, the actor who played the monster. Several other actors turned down the part when they learned that the monster would not get to speak any lines and that his face would be covered with heavy makeup. But Karloff realized that "That Monster is one of the most sympathetic characters ever created in the world of English letters."

Karloff stressed the childlike nature of the monster: his

Boris Karloff relaxing at home with his dogs

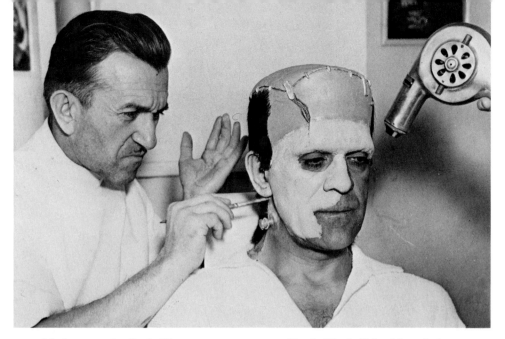

Makeup artist Jack Pierce prepares actor Boris Karloff for his role in *Son of Frankenstein.*

delight in sunlight, his fear of fire, his playful innocence with the little girl Maria, whom he kills accidentally. Makeup artist Jack Pierce made sure that the mask he designed for the monster only came down as far as Karloff's eyebrows. That way, the actor could still make full use of his expressive eyes and mouth. Karloff's awkward movements were partly the result of a heavy rod running up his spine, which kept his back rigid, and boots that weighed 13 pounds (5.9 kilograms) each.

Boris Karloff played the monster again in *The Bride of Frankenstein* (1935) and *Son of Frankenstein* (1939). He was proud of the role he had created. He once remarked that thousands of children had written to him over the years, "expressing compassion for the great, weird creature who was so abused by its sadistic keeper that it could only respond to violence with violence. These children saw beyond the makeup and really understood."

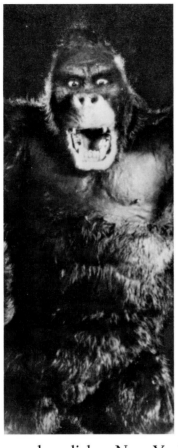

(1933)

# KING KONG

*b/w*
*dir/pro* Merian C. Cooper, Ernest
      B. Schoedsack
*st* Fay Wray, Robert Armstrong
*sp eff* Willis O'Brien

**M**onster movies often tell the same story in different ways. A giant shark invades a popular beach resort. A huge ape demolishes New York City. A dinosaur destroys Tokyo.

In many of these stories, the world in which people live is shown as a very confusing place. Science and machines have taken over people's lives. People are crowded together in big cities. Everyone has to follow many different laws and rules. By contrast, monsters seem to stand for a way of life that is simple, powerful, and free.

In the 1933 movie *King Kong*, a giant gorilla stomped across New York City. Then he climbed the world's tallest building and fought with airplanes that were trying to kill him. Audiences did not cheer for the airplanes. They cheered for the giant gorilla. The gorilla was fighting for his freedom. He was fighting against the danger and confusion of the modern world.

## "It Was Beauty Killed the Beast"

Carl Denham is a filmmaker with a great idea for a new movie. Its theme will be "Beauty and the Beast," the story of a beautiful woman and a frightening monster.

Denham thinks he knows where he can find a monster, but he is having trouble finding an actress to star in his film. Driving around New York City one night, Denham sees Ann Darrow, a hungry, out-of-work actress. The Great Depression has struck the country, and many Americans do not have much money or jobs. Ann is about to steal an apple from a fruit stand when Denham approaches her. He takes her to a restaurant, buys her a meal, and tells her about his movie idea.

"It's money and adventure and fame," he promises. "It's the thrill of a lifetime and a long sea voyage that starts at six o'clock tomorrow morning." Ann agrees to star in Denham's film. The next day, they leave New York on a ship bound for the South Pacific.

Aboard the ship, First Mate Jack Driscoll becomes upset with Denham. Jack says it is wrong to bring a woman on such a dangerous voyage. In fact, Jack is falling in love with Ann and doesn't want to admit it.

Near the end of the voyage, Carl Denham shows the men a secret map of Skull Island in the East Indies. Skull Island, Denham says, is surrounded by steep cliffs. There is only one entrance to the main part of the island. Long ago, the island's natives built a towering wall to block off that entrance. "There's something on the other side of the wall," Denham says. "Something they fear."

Skull Island natives prepare to sacrifice Ann.

When Denham and his crew land on Skull Island, they find the natives holding a strange ceremony. Men dressed as gorillas are dancing around a young girl, who is being prepared for some sort of sacrifice. The natives chant "Kong, Kong," over and over.

While his crew hides behind some bushes, Carl Denham sets up his movie camera to film the ceremony. The native chief sees Denham filming. Angry at being spied on, the chief stops the ceremony. He shouts at the visitors to leave at once. Denham's men ready their rifles as fierce, spear-waving natives come closer and closer.

Suddenly, the chief commands his warriors to stop. He has just noticed Ann hiding behind Jack Driscoll. The chief has never seen a white woman before. He offers to buy Ann, but Denham refuses. Holding their rifles steady, Denham and his crew retreat to the safety of their ship.

That night, natives sneak on board the ship and kidnap Ann. Before the crew realizes Ann is missing, the natives have taken her ashore and prepared her for sacrifice. The native warriors open a tall gate in the huge wall. They take Ann inside and leave her tied to a post. Then the natives climb to the top of the wall to watch what happens next.

As Ann struggles to escape, she hears horrible roars and the sound of some giant beast crashing through the jungle. Then she sees the monster: an unbelievably huge gorilla, bigger than a house, towering above the trees. Ann screams in terror. King Kong beats his chest and roars. Then he comes closer and looks at Ann curiously.

After shaking several men from a tree bridge to their deaths, King Kong battles a Tyrannosaurus rex, a lizard, and finally a Pterodactyl.

Kong picks up Ann in his giant paw and carries her off into the jungle.

Carl Denham and Jack Driscoll arrive too late to save Ann. They lead a rescue party through the open gate and into the thick jungle. There the men are attacked by dinosaurs and use guns and gas bombs to fight them.

Up ahead, Kong hears the men chasing him. He sets Ann down on a tree branch and walks back to see what is happening. Kong finds several of the men crossing a deep ravine, using a fallen tree as a bridge. The powerful ape picks up the tree-bridge and shakes it, sending the men falling to their deaths. Only Denham and Jack Driscoll survive. Jack tells Denham to go for help while he follows Kong and Ann.

Kong fights a tremendous battle with a Tyrannosaurus rex and later kills a huge lizard that tries to eat Ann. The gorilla not only protects his captive, but he also seems to be falling in love with her. While Kong is fighting a winged Pterodactyl, however, Jack Driscoll rescues Ann. The two of them jump off a cliff into the water far below.

Jack and Ann return safely to the native village with Kong following close behind. Kong breaks down the huge gate that has kept him trapped inside the island. He smashes the village, biting, stomping, and crushing the natives. Before he can reach Ann and Jack, however, Kong is knocked out by one of Carl Denham's gas bombs.

Denham persuades the crew to help him take Kong back to the United States. By charging money to see the giant gorilla, Denham says, they all will become rich.

Back in New York City, Denham sells tickets to see King Kong in chains, "the Eighth Wonder of the World." On opening night, Denham invites Jack and Ann to come onstage while newspaper reporters take pictures of King Kong. The photographers' flashbulbs frighten and anger the mighty ape. Kong thinks the popping lights are guns being fired at Ann, the woman he loves. Breaking free of his chains, Kong smashes his way out of the theater. He later finds Ann and carries her across New York City. Holding her in his giant paw, he climbs New York's tallest building, the Empire State Building.

Carl Denham calls for airplanes to shoot King Kong. Kong sets Ann on a ledge of the Empire State Building, high above the city. He tries to grab the planes, and even sends one pilot to a fiery death. But the planes' machine guns are too much for King Kong. Finally, he is wounded so badly that he can no longer hang onto the building. The great King Kong falls to his death.

On the ground below, Carl Denham looks at the lifeless body of King Kong. "Well, the airplanes got him," says a policeman. Denham, still thinking of the story he first set

In New York, Carl Denham advertises King Kong as the "Eighth
Wonder of the World," but the gorilla soon breaks free of his chains.

out to tell, shakes his head. "No," he says. "It wasn't airplanes. It was Beauty killed the Beast."

## AN ADVENTURER AND A MAGICIAN

Two men were most responsible for the making of *King Kong.* One was an adventurous movie producer named Merian C. Cooper. The other was a Hollywood movie magician named Willis O'Brien.

Merian Cooper loved danger. As a young man, he was shot down while flying combat airplanes in World War I. (Cooper himself flew one of the airplanes that attacked King Kong in the movie.) During the 1920s, Cooper filmed movies in remote parts of Africa and Asia. The character Carl Denham in *King Kong* is modeled after Merian C. Cooper.

When he was a boy, Cooper heard a story that fascinated him. It was about a giant gorilla who kidnapped a young woman. When he became a movie producer, Cooper got the chance to tell this story. There was one problem, however. Merian Cooper did not know how to bring a giant gorilla to life.

Then Cooper saw a short film called *Creation* by a Hollywood special effects technician named Willis O'Brien. In *Creation*, giant dinosaurs roamed through dense jungles, battling each other and the men who invaded their land. Cooper was surprised by how real the dinosaurs looked. Living men and extinct monsters seemed to have been captured on film together.

To accomplish this trick, Willis O'Brien built small models of his dinosaurs. He placed them in tiny model jungles. Then he brought the models to life through a camera trick called *stop-motion animation*. This involved stopping and starting the movie camera many times. Each time the camera stopped, O'Brien changed the position of his models slightly. Then he turned the camera back on and filmed the models in a new position. When O'Brien showed his finished film, the models seemed to be moving by themselves. Later, pictures of live actors were sandwiched together with these shots of dinosaurs.

Merian Cooper asked O'Brien to use his movie magic to create King Kong. For some scenes, O'Brien and Cooper used a huge hand or head of Kong so Ann Darrow (played by actress Fay Wray) could be shown screaming in closeup.

Merian C. Cooper wrote, directed, and produced *King Kong*, considered one the world's classic monster movies.

The rest of the time, however, King Kong was one of Willis O'Brien's tiny models, only 18 inches (45 centimeters) tall.

In 1976, Hollywood filmmakers decided to remake *King Kong*. This time they built a full-sized monster, which stood 40 feet (12 meters) tall and weighed 6½ tons (585 kg). In the opinion of many viewers, however, the new Kong was neither as frightening nor as believable as the tiny monster that Merian Cooper and Willis O'Brien had created 40 years earlier.

An artist draws sketches of gorillas for the 1976 remake of *King Kong*.

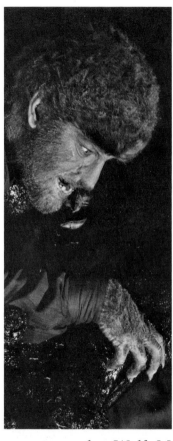

# THE WOLF MAN

*b/w*
*pro/dir* George Waggner
*st* Lon Chaney, Jr., Claude Rains,
   Ralph Bellamy, Evelyn Ankers
*makeup* Jack Pierce

The Wolf Man is a tragic character, a man who turns into a monster through no fault of his own. Like many movie monsters, the Wolf Man cannot control what he does. Even as he frightens us, he makes us feel sorry for him. Other characters also seem to feel sympathy for him. Many characters recite a poem to the Wolf Man:

> *Even a man who is pure in heart*
> *and says his prayers by night*
> *may become a wolf when the wolfsbane blooms*
> *and the autumn moon is bright.*

## "There's a Werewolf in Camp"

Larry Talbot has just returned to Wales after working

in America for 18 years. His father, Sir John Talbot, has asked Larry to come home and help run Talbot Castle, the family estate.

Sir John asks Larry to help him install a new lens in a giant telescope he has built in the attic. Testing the lens, Larry scans the local village and spies a beautiful young woman in an apartment above an antique store. That afternoon, he visits the store and asks the young woman, whose name is Gwen, for a date.

While talking with Gwen, Larry sees a cane with a silver handle in the shape of a wolf. On the side of the handle is a pentagram, a five-pointed star. Larry asks Gwen what the star means.

Gwen tells Larry that the pentagram is the mark of the werewolf—a man who turns into a wolf "when the wolfsbane blooms and the autumn moon is bright." Sometimes a werewolf sees a pentagram in the palm of his next victim's hand.

Larry laughs at the idea of werewolves. He buys the cane and leaves the shop, promising Gwen he will come back for a date that evening. As he leaves, two gypsy wagons roll through town. Gwen tells Larry that the gypsies are fortune tellers.

That night, Gwen is waiting outside the shop for Larry. Since she does not know Larry very well, she has asked her friend Jenny to come along on their date. Together, the three of them walk through the dark woods to the gypsy camp. Along the way, Jenny finds a sprig of wolfsbane, a plant that is supposed to keep away werewolves. She too recites the poem about a man "pure in heart" turning into a wolf. Larry thinks it is funny that everyone in the village seems to know that poem.

At the gypsy camp, Jenny asks to have her fortune told

At the antique shop, Gwen shows Larry the pentagram sign on a cane.

first. A gypsy man named Bela takes Jenny into his tent while Gwen and Larry stroll into the foggy night.

Inside the gypsy's tent, Bela tries to tell Jenny's fortune, but he becomes more and more upset. He throws Jenny's sprig of wolfsbane on the ground. Finally, Bela asks to see Jenny's hands. "Your left hand shows your past," he says. "Your right hand shows your future." In the palm of Jenny's right hand, Bela sees a pentagram, the mark of a werewolf's next victim. "Go away," he tells her. "Go quickly."

Jenny does not know why Bela is so upset, but she is

frightened. She runs out of the camp into the foggy night. Off in the woods, Larry and Gwen hear a wolf howling. Then they hear Jenny scream. Larry rushes to help her. He sees her on the ground, being attacked by a fierce wolf. Larry pulls the wolf off Jenny and beats it to death with his silver-handled cane.

Gwen rushes up to find Jenny lying dead. Larry has been badly bitten. Gwen calls out to Maleva, Bela's mother. The old gypsy woman brings a horse-drawn wagon, and they take Larry back to Talbot Castle.

Captain Paul Montford, the head of the local police force, examines the scene of Jenny's death. He is sure that Jenny was killed by some large animal, but he does not believe in werewolves. Near Jenny's body lies Bela the gypsy, who seems to have been beaten to death. Montford discovers wolf tracks around the bodies and, not far away, he finds Larry's silver-handled cane.

The next morning, Montford and the town doctor visit Talbot Castle. When they ask Larry about the killings, he admits that the cane is his, but he cannot explain how Bela was killed. He insists, "I saw only a wolf." However, when he shows the doctor the place where the wolf bit him, there is only the faint sign of a pentagram.

Larry walks into town and visits the chapel where Bela's body is resting. He overhears Maleva tell the local priest that many gypsies are coming to town to give her son a special funeral. After Maleva leaves, Larry leans on the coffin of the man whom everyone thinks he killed. He weeps in helpless grief.

That night, the gypsies hold a celebration for Bela, dancing and playing violins. Bela's mother takes Larry aside and tells him that the wolf he killed was Bela. "Whoever is bitten by a werewolf and lives," Maleva says, "becomes a werewolf himself." She gives Larry a pentagram charm and tells him to wear it over his heart always. Outside, Larry gives the charm to Gwen, "just in case."

Maleva whispers something to one of the gypsies, and soon all the gypsies are whispering to each other and packing up their wagons. When Larry asks what is going on, a gypsy tells him, "There's a werewolf in camp."

Alone in his room that night, Larry feels a change coming over him. He examines his hands, his arms, his chest, and his face, but sees nothing. Then he takes off his shoes and sees thick wolf's hair sprouting on his feet and legs.

Out in the woods, a gravedigger has just finished burying Bela. As he wipes the sweat off his brow, he glances up and sees a terrifying figure moving towards him. It walks on two legs and wears clothes like a man, but it is covered with hair and has the wild eyes, pointed ears, and sharp teeth of a wolf. Before the gravedigger can scream, the Wolf Man springs forward and bites his neck.

The next morning, Larry finds muddy wolf tracks leading right up to his bedroom window. He tries to tell his father that he thinks he turned into a werewolf. Sir John does not believe in werewolves. He thinks his son is having a mental breakdown. He tells Larry, "I do believe that most anything can happen to a man in his own mind."

The next night, the Wolf Man prowls again. He steps in a hidden trap planted by Frank Andrews, the Talbots' gamekeeper. The sharp teeth of the trap bite into the Wolf Man's hairy leg, and he rolls on the ground in pain. Maleva, the old gypsy woman, finds him and prays over him. The Wolf Man changes back into Larry Talbot, who frees himself from the trap and escapes before Frank Andrews and his men can capture him.

Will Gwen escape the Wolf Man?

Larry hurries to the antique shop to tell Gwen he is leaving the village. He tells her he is a murderer, but she doesn't believe him. As Larry takes Gwen's hand to say goodbye, he sees a pentagram in her palm. She will be his next victim.

The next night, Larry's father refuses to let him leave the castle. Sir John ties Larry to a chair and locks the doors and windows of his room. He wants his son to realize that he only *thinks* he is a werewolf. As Sir John leaves to join the party hunting the "real" wolf, Larry begs him to take along the silver-handled cane.

Men with torches and guns prowl the woods that night, looking for the wolf. Gwen rushes toward the castle, hoping to help Larry.

Suddenly Sir John hears screams. The Wolf Man is attacking Gwen. Sir John races to her rescue. He beats the Wolf Man with the silver-handled cane over and over again.

As the Wolf Man lies still on the ground, the old gypsy Maleva arrives in her wagon. She approaches and kneels by the body. "Your suffering is over," she says. "Now you will find peace for eternity." As she speaks, Sir John sees the Wolf Man turning back into his son Larry.

Frank Andrews rushes up to Gwen and makes sure she is all right. Captain Montford tries to comfort Sir John. "The wolf must have attacked her," he says, "and Larry came to the rescue. I'm sorry, Sir John." They all know that Captain Montford's story is not the truth.

"Your suffering is over," the old gypsy tells the Wolf Man.

Lon Chaney, Sr.

Lon Chaney, Jr.

# THE SON OF THE MAN
# OF A THOUSAND FACES

In *The Wolf Man*, Larry Talbot had a hard time living up to his father's reputation. While Sir John was a brilliant scientist and a leader in his community, Larry was just a simple man. He was good with tools, but not too smart.

In real life, the actor who played Larry, Lon Chaney, Jr., also had a difficult time following in his father's footsteps. Chaney's father, Lon Chaney, Sr., was the most famous horror movie actor of all time. In the 1920s, he was known as "the Man of a Thousand Faces" because of the many scary characters he portrayed.

Lon Chaney, Jr., whose real name was Creighton Chaney, wanted to be an actor like his father, but his father discouraged him. As a result, Creighton left school, got married, and went to work for a water heater company. It was not until after his father died in 1930 that Creighton began to act in motion pictures.

The Hollywood studios wanted Creighton to change his name so audiences would know that he was the son of the famous actor. For a long time, he refused to do it, and for a long time, the studios refused to hire him. Finally, in 1937, Creighton changed his name to Lon Chaney, Jr. He began to win important movie roles, and within two years, he became a star. He went on to play the Wolf Man in several more films, including *Frankenstein Meets the Wolf Man*, *House of Dracula*, and *Abbott and Costello Meet Frankenstein*.

# GODZILLA

*b/w*
*pro* Tomoyuki Tanaka
*dir* Inshiro Honda
*st* Raymond Burr, Haru Nakajima,
    Takaski Shimura, Momoka
    Kachi
*sp eff* Eiji Tsuburaya

Godzilla is a Japanese film monster who has been called the most popular movie monster of all time. He has appeared in more than a dozen films. Four hundred feet (120 m) tall, Godzilla is a beast from the age of dinosaurs. He walks upright like a Tyrannosaurus rex, and he has sharp scales on his back like a Stegosaurus. Guns, bombs, and high-tension electric wires do not kill Godzilla. Stomping through cities like Tokyo, he destroys everything in his path.

*"Neither Man Nor His Machines
Are Able to Stop This Creature"*

Steve Martin, a United States newspaperman, has come to Tokyo to visit a scientist friend, Dr. Serazawa. Arriving

**Raymond Burr** *(center)* **plays Steve Martin in** *Godzilla.*

at the airport, Steve learns that a ship has been destroyed at sea, just off the coast of Japan. The ship's few survivors tell of a blinding flash of light. This flash caused the ocean to boil and the ship to burst into flames.

Before long, more ships are blown up. At a meeting of Japanese scientists in Tokyo, Dr. Yamane gets up to speak. He suggests that a party of scientists be sent to Odo Island, which is near the spot where the ships were destroyed. The Odo Island natives, Dr. Yamane says, believe that a great sea monster named Godzilla lives in their waters.

Steve Martin gets permission to accompany Dr. Yamane to Odo Island. There they find gigantic holes in the ground, which Dr. Yamane says are the footprints of a living creature.

Suddenly a gong alarm is sounded by a lookout on a hill. Steve, Dr. Yamane, and the villagers race to the top of the hill. From there they see the huge, horrible head of Godzilla, rising up as high as the hilltop. The monster walks back into the sea, though. For the time being, everyone is safe.

Back in Tokyo, Dr. Yamane describes Godzilla to his fellow scientists. The doctor says that nuclear bomb tests awakened Godzilla from millions of years of sleep. The bomb blasts also made Godzilla's breath radioactive, so anything the creature breathes on will burst into flames.

**Godzilla rises out of Tokyo Bay.**

Dr. Yamane's daughter, Emiko, is engaged to marry Steve's friend, Dr. Serazawa. Dr. Serazawa is a mysterious figure who conducts strange experiments that seem to make him very unhappy.

Emiko tells Dr. Serazawa that she cannot marry him because she loves a young sailor. Angry with her, the doctor shows her something terrible. He has invented an "Oxygen Destroyer," a kind of bomb that will kill anything that lives in water. Dr. Serazawa warns Emiko, "The world must not know of this."

Meanwhile, out in Tokyo Bay, the Japanese navy drops bombs into the water to kill Godzilla. Everyone is sure the monster has been destroyed. That night, however, Godzilla rises out of the water and walks into Tokyo.

Godzilla towers over buildings and crushes everything in his path. He steps on a railroad track, causing a horrible train wreck. Even a powerful electric fence strung around the city cannot stop Godzilla. Godzilla rips up the high-tension wires and melts the electrical towers with his radioactive breath.

As Godzilla marches across Tokyo, Steve Martin speaks into a tape recorder, describing the city's destruction. He says, "Neither man nor his machines are able to stop this creature. Godzilla has turned the heart of Tokyo into a sea of fire."

Godzilla smashes the building Steve is in, and Steve is crushed beneath the rubble. Miraculously, he survives. The next day, after Godzilla has returned to the ocean, Emiko finds Steve in the hospital. She tells him about Dr. Serazawa's Oxygen Destroyer. A bomb no larger than a baseball, she tells Steve, will destroy all life in Tokyo Bay.

Dr. Serazawa finally is persuaded to use his invention

against Godzilla, but he burns his formula to prevent anyone from ever using it again. As Steve, Emiko, and Dr. Yamane watch from a ship in Tokyo Bay, Dr. Serazawa puts on a diving suit and jumps into the water. Under the water, he confronts Godzilla and sets off his Oxygen Destroyer. As the water boils around Godzilla, the monster is reduced to a skeleton.

Serazawa decides not to return to the surface. He cuts his oxygen line and dies with Godzilla. This is his way of making sure that his terrible weapon will never be used again. Steve says, "The menace was gone, but so was a great man. The whole world could wake up and live again."

## FROM VILLAIN TO HERO

Although Godzilla died at the end of his first movie, he was so popular with audiences that Japan's Toho Studios decided to bring him back for more films. New movie monsters like Mothra (a giant moth) and Rodan (a flying prehistoric monster) were created to do battle with Godzilla. In the 1962 film *King Kong Vs. Godzilla*, the two greatest movie monsters of all time fought to a standoff.

It was in *King Kong Vs. Godzilla* that Godzilla began to develop a comic personality. He made fun of King Kong, rolling his eyes and even holding his belly while laughing.

Godzilla's gestures and his characteristic way of moving were created by a good-natured actor named Haru Nakajima. To play the role of Godzilla, Nakajima wore a rubber reptile suit that weighed 100 pounds (45 kg). In this big, heavy suit, Nakajima stomped across model streets and buildings designed to look like the city of Tokyo. Two small Godzilla models also were used for some scenes. One of them was specially equipped to spray Godzilla's smoky atomic breath.

Ghidrah, the three-headed monster, came from outer space and fought with Godzilla.

In the 1965 film *Ghidrah, The Three-Headed Monster*, the people of Japan called on Godzilla to save them from a horrible monster from outer space. With the help of Mothra and Rodan, Godzilla drove the alien creature Ghidrah back into outer space. From this film on, Godzilla usually appeared as a hero who saved Japan from other monsters and space creatures.

Many film critics feel that Godzilla has a special meaning for the Japanese people. Japan is the only country ever to suffer the effects of an atomic bomb explosion. More than 200,000 Japanese people were killed by two atomic bomb blasts in 1945.

For the Japanese, Godzilla seems to represent the horrible power of the atomic age. Unless that power is controlled, it might someday destroy everyone on Earth.

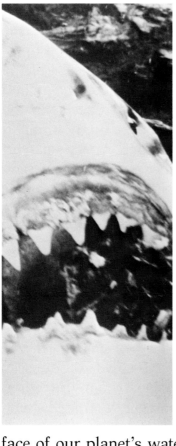

# JAWS

*color*
*dir* Steven Spielberg
*pro* Richard D. Zanuck, David
  Brown
*st* Roy Scheider, Robert Shaw,
  Richard Dreyfuss, Lorraine
  Gary
*sp eff* Robert Mattey

The 1975 movie *Jaws* tapped into a very basic human fear: the fear of what might be lurking just below the dark surface of our planet's waters. *Jaws* was the inspiraton for a flood of underwater monster movies, including *Piranha* (a film about vicious fish), *Orca* (a killer whale), *Alligator*, and of course, several sequels to *Jaws* itself, including *Jaws 3-D*, in which the shark seemed to pop right off the screen at the audience.

## "This Shark'll Swallow You Whole"

Chrissie will never go swimming again. The teenager goes for a late-night dip in the waters off Amity Island, a resort community in Massachusetts. The next morning,

Police Chief Martin Brody finds the remains of Chrissie's body washed up on the beach. The sight nearly makes him sick. Most of Chrissie's body has been chewed up.

Chief Brody is new to Amity Island. In the eyes of the locals, he is an outsider, someone who does not understand how things are done. When the local coroner tells the chief that Chrissie was killed by a shark, Brody immediately decides to close the island's beaches. Amity's mayor, Larry Vaughn, tells Brody that the beaches must stay open. All the businesses in town depend on summer tourists. If the beaches are closed—particularly because of a shark attack—the tourists will stay away.

The beaches stay open, but Chief Brody is worried. He sits in the sand, frantically scanning the shore, where hundreds of happy bathers frolic in the surf. Chief Brody himself doesn't like the water. He doesn't swim, and he doesn't go out on boats.

Just beyond most of the bathers, a boy named Alex is floating on a rubber raft. Suddenly, Chief Brody sees something that makes his eyes pop. A giant fin slices through the water and, just for a moment, a strange shape surfaces beneath Alex's raft. As it does, Alex seems to explode, gushing blood like a fire hydrant. As terrified parents pull their children out of the water, Chief Brody runs along the beach. Alex's mother calls his name over and over. The boy's rubber raft washes ashore at her feet. A gaping hole has been bitten out of it.

The next day, the Amity City Council meets to talk about closing the beaches. In the middle of the meeting, everyone is silenced by a horrible screeching sound coming from the rear of the room. Quint, a grizzled old shark hunter, is dragging his fingernails along a blackboard to get everyone's attention.

It's not safe to swim in the waters off Amity Island.

"You all know me," Quint says. "You know how I make a living. I'll catch this bird for you. Ain't going to be easy. Bad fish. This shark'll swallow you whole." Quint offers to kill the shark for $10,000. The mayor turns him down.

Alex's mother has offered a $3,000 reward to any fisherman who can kill the shark. Soon dozens of shark hunters arrive, and one of them catches a huge shark. Everyone rushes to the dock to see it. Mayor Vaughn says the crisis is over. Chief Brody happily poses for pictures with the triumphant fisherman. But Matt Hooper takes the chief aside and tells him there is a problem.

Hooper is a research scientist who has just arrived in Amity. He has examined the body of the shark's first victim, Chrissie, and he tells the chief that he is certain Chrissie was killed by a different shark.

**Chief Brody** *(center)* **and Matt Hooper** *(right)* **try to persuade the mayor of Amity Island to close the beaches.**

Chief Brody has a dilemma. The mayor and the towns-people are rejoicing because they think the shark has been killed. Thousands of people are coming to the island for the Fourth of July holiday. Now this young, hotshot scientist tells him that everyone else is wrong. A rogue shark lives in the waters off Amity Island. It will eat anything that moves, and it most commonly attacks swimmers in only 3 feet of water, 10 feet from the beach. "What we are dealing with here," says Hooper, "is a perfect engine: an eating machine."

As Chief Brody wonders what he should do, Alex's mother approaches him. Dressed in black with a veil over her face, she fights to hold back her tears. She looks right at Chief Brody and slaps him across the face. She says her boy would still be alive if the chief had closed the beaches after the first shark attack. Brody stares at the ground, feeling miserable, knowing that she is right.

No amount of arguing, however, will convince the mayor to close the beaches on the Fourth of July. As tourists splash in the water, boats and helicopters patrol the shore. One boat spots a giant shark swimming straight into a group of bathers. The swimmers run screaming to the

Hundreds of beachgoers panic when a (fake) shark is spotted.

shore, but the "shark" is merely a large cardboard fin propelled by two boys wearing swim masks and snorkels. Everyone is nervously laughing at this prank when they see another dark fin cutting through the water, moving towards a group of boys in a sailboat. One of the boys is Chief Brody's son Michael.

By the time the chief reaches his son, the shark has bitten off another boy's leg and headed back to sea. Michael is pulled to shore safely, but he is in shock. After taking his son to the hospital, Brody grabs Mayor Vaughn and demands that he sign a money order for $10,000. It is time to hire Quint to kill the shark. The mayor, shaken by what has happened, scribbles his signature on the piece of paper.

The next morning, Chief Brody and Matt Hooper visit Quint's shack. The shack's walls are lined with the jaws of sharks that Quint has killed. Quint reluctantly agrees to let the two men accompany him, but he makes it clear that he is the captain.

Once at sea, Chief Brody ends up having to do all the dirty work, while Quint fishes and Hooper drives the boat. The worst job is "chumming," throwing spoiled, bloody meat over the side of the boat to attract the shark. As the chief scoops out a bucketful of slop, a monstrous shark rises out of the water and nearly takes his hand off. Brody cannot believe the size of the creature he has just seen. "You're going to need a bigger boat," Brody tells Quint.

Even Quint is awestruck by the size of the shark. He estimates it to be 25 feet long, weighing 3 tons—about the size of a car pulling a small trailer. Using a special rifle, Quint fires a harpoon into the side of the beast. Attached to the harpoon by a long rope is a heavy yellow

Quint feels an enormous pull on his line as Brody watches tensely.

barrel. Pulling the barrel through the water, Quint says, will tire the shark out sooner or later.

In the meantime, the three men sit in the boat's cabin and swap tales of their adventures. Quint's story is the most terrifying. During World War II, he served as a sailor. His ship was sunk by a Japanese submarine, and 1,100 men went into the water. Five days later, when the survivors were rescued, only 316 men were still alive. Sharks ate the rest. Quint was one of the survivors, but the experience scarred him for life.

Just as Quint finishes his story, the shark attacks, pounding the hull of the boat, flooding the engine, and knocking out the lights. Brody and Hooper realize that their mission is far more dangerous than they ever anticipated. But Quint seems almost gleeful, delighted by the opportunity to kill the biggest shark of his career. When Brody attempts to radio the Coast Guard for help, Quint smashes the radio. The chief is beginning to wonder if Quint is crazy.

The men battle the shark, harpooning it with two more barrels, but their boat is beginning to sink. In desperation, Quint agrees to let Hooper dive overboard in a protective shark cage and attempt to spear the monster with a poison dart. Under the water, Hooper fails to spot the shark coming up behind him. The beast knocks the spear out of Hooper's hands, then rips the cage apart. Hooper is able to swim free and hide behind a rock underwater, however.

The shark turns his attention to the boat, rising out of the water and smashing down on its bow. Screaming and struggling, Quint slides into the open jaws of the monster.

Brody locks himself in the boat's cabin, but the shark smashes through the cabin wall. With a tremendous heave,

Brody flings an oxygen tank into the shark's mouth. The shark swims away, circles, and rushes toward the boat to make its final kill. Brody grabs a rifle and climbs out on the sinking boat's mast, which now juts out only a few feet above the water. Firing shot after shot, Brody watches the jaws of death hurtling toward him. With one last desperate effort, Brody takes aim at the oxygen tank lodged in the monster's mouth and pulls the trigger. The tank explodes and the shark is blown to pieces.

Matt Hooper swims to the surface. When Brody sees Hooper, whom he thought was dead, he shakes his head and laughs. Together, the two men paddle toward shore on the floating yellow barrels. "I used to hate the water," Brody says.

"I can't imagine why," replies Hooper.

## THE SAGA OF "BRUCE"

*Jaws* was originally scheduled to be filmed in 52 days at the resort town of Martha's Vineyard in Massachusetts. The actual filming took three times as long. The film crew began to feel that they, too, were victims of the mechanical shark they nicknamed "Bruce" (supposedly in honor of director Steven Spielberg's attorney). Hour after hour, the crew struggled to make the 24-foot-long (720 cm) shark move through the water in a believable fashion.

Actually, three full-sized models of "Bruce" were built: one that could be filmed from the left side, one for filming from the right side, and one for head-on shots. The left-side and right-side models were bare on the side away from the camera so that the crew could more easily reach the complex machinery that made the shark swim, dive, and lunge. The shark models were built by a special effects technician named Bob Mattey. Seventeen years earlier,

Mattey had constructed the giant squid for Walt Disney's film *20,000 Leagues Under the Sea.*

For the scene in which Matt Hooper goes underwater in a protective cage, a real great white shark was used. This real shark was much smaller than the giant mechanical shark used for other scenes, so a midget actor played Matt Hooper. When seen alongside the midget, the real shark looked as huge as the mechanical one.

*Jaws* became one of the blockbuster movie hits of all time. In spite of the film's success, director Spielberg says that if he were to make the film again, he would not show the shark. Instead, he would let the monster take shape in the imaginations of the audience.

After *Jaws*, director Steven Spielberg made many successful movies, including *E.T.*

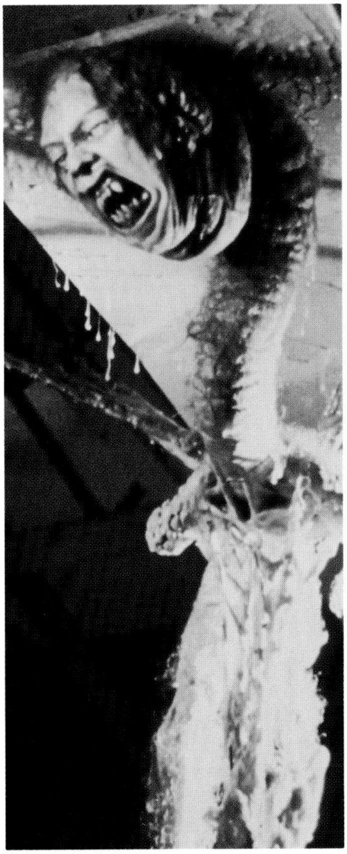

# THE THING

*color*
*dir* John Carpenter
*pro* David Foster,
    Lawrence Turman
*co-producer* Stuart Cohen
*st* Kurt Russell, A. Wilford
    Brimley, T.K. Carter
*makeup* Rob Bottin

**S**ome monster movies are frightening because the monsters are hidden most of the time. These movies let viewers' imaginations take over. They let viewers wonder what the monster will look like. This was the approach filmmakers first took when *The Thing* was made into a movie in 1951.

Other monster movies show huge, scary-looking creatures. Director John Carpenter decided to adopt this approach when he remade *The Thing* in 1982. In his version of the film, the Thing became one of the most horrifying movie monsters of all time.

### "I Know I'm Human"

*The Thing* opens with a startling scene. A beautiful

59

**MacReady** *(second from left)* **and the others watch a videotape that the Norwegians left behind.**

black and white husky dog is running through the deep snow fields of Antarctica. Suddenly a helicopter appears. Men inside the helicopter are shooting at the dog, trying to kill it for no apparent reason. To escape the men in the helicopter, the dog races toward a low group of buildings. A sign identifies the buildings as a research station for U.S. scientists.

The Americans rush outside to rescue the dog. As they do so, the men in the helicopter accidentally blow themselves up. The Americans have no idea what made these men—whom they recognize as scientists from Norway—act so crazily.

One of the Americans, "Mac" MacReady, is the man the others count on when trouble arises. MacReady decides to find out why the Norwegians were chasing the dog. He flies the camp helicopter to the Norwegian research station, where he makes an amazing discovery: a huge block of ice with a large hole cut out of it. Apparently the Norwegian scientists found someone—or something—frozen in the ice. Whatever it was, it is gone now.

Mac also finds the body of a dead Norwegian scientist. Back at the U.S. research station, a dozen men look on as Mac shows them the Norwegian's body. The body's face has been twisted into a shape that looks barely human.

Two of the older scientists, Doc Copper and a grouchy but kindly man named Blair, cut open the body to see what killed it. Blair is fascinated by what he finds. The body seems to be human and yet not human at the same time. He wants to study it further.

Meanwhile, the dog that the men saved earlier is placed in a pen with the camp's other dogs. The new dog turns into a monster. Legs like a giant spider's legs sprout right out of its sides. Dozens of tentacles pop out of different parts of the dog's body. The tentacles dart out to attack anything they can reach. Mac yells for someone to bring a flamethrower, and the men destroy the monster.

Back inside, Blair explains to the other men how the monster works. It gets inside its victim, then begins to imitate the victim. Before long, the monster looks just like the dog—or person—it has invaded. What the monster wants to do next, says Blair, is to take over each and every one of the men, slowly and silently.

This is just what begins to happen. The monster has already moved from the dog into one of the men. Soon it attacks the others. Fear turns the men against each other. No one knows who is human and who is a monster. Blair goes crazy and destroys the camp's radio. Only MacReady is able to restore order. He locks Blair in a toolshed and gathers the other men together.

"I know I'm human," Mac says. "And if you were all these 'things,' you'd attack me right now. So some of you

62

MacReady gets ready to destroy the Thing.

must be human, too." The problem for MacReady is to figure out who is human, and who is a monster.

Mac invents a blood test that will determine who is human. Before he can use it, though, a scientist named Norris suffers a heart attack. As Doc Copper works to save Norris's life, the monster suddenly bursts out of Norris's chest. It bites off both of Doc Copper's arms. Then before MacReady can light his flamethrower, the Norris-monster sprouts a new head. It rises to the ceiling on a long, dragon-like neck. Meanwhile, Norris's own head has grown spider's legs and is running around on the floor.

MacReady lights his flamethrower just in time and kills the Norris-monster. Then he uses his blood test to show that he and four other men are really human beings, not monsters. Blair, however, has been taken over by the

**Special effects wizard Rob Bottin** *(in makeup)* **demonstrates the scary Thing he created.**

monster. Not only that, he has escaped from the toolshed and destroyed the camp's power supply. The only way to kill him now is to blow up the entire camp.

In a final, gruesome battle, MacReady destroys the Blair-monster. In the end, Blair looks like a huge, bald, slimy, two-headed dog. When the battle is over, only MacReady and one other man are left alive. Neither man is sure whether or not the monster has taken over the other man. But they are both too tired to do anything about it. As the camp burns, the two men sink down into the snow. They wait for the cold Antarctic winter to come and cover them.

# A 24-YEAR-OLD WIZARD

The Thing first appeared in a 1938 short story called "Who Goes There?" by Don Stuart. In this story, scientists in Antarctica discover a monster from another planet buried beneath the ice. The monster stands four feet (120 cm) tall and has blue hair and green blood. Instead of arms, it has tentacles like an octopus. Three angry red eyes glow in its face.

**Rob Bottin with friend**

The original movie version of *The Thing* was released in 1951.

"Who Goes There?" has twice been made into a film called *The Thing.* In the first version, filmed in 1951, the monster was larger than in Don Stuart's story. It stood nearly seven feet (210 cm) tall and had huge claws and a giant, bald head. In most other ways, however, this Thing looked like a large human being. Played by actor James Arness, the early Thing looked a lot like Frankenstein's monster.

In 1982, director John Carpenter decided to remake *The*

*Thing* as a much scarier-looking monster. His version of *The Thing* is the story you have just read.

Carpenter hired a young makeup wizard named Rob Bottin to design the rubber masks and models that made the "Thing" look real. Bottin was only 24 years old, but he had been designing movie makeup for 10 years. As a freshman in high school, Bottin made a deal with his teachers. He would come to class in the morning if they would let him work on movies in the afternoon. Bottin's first job in the movies involved sewing hair onto the giant ape costumes used for the 1976 remake of *King Kong*.

For the new version of *The Thing*, Bottin and his 40-member crew designed some of the strangest monsters ever seen on a movie screen. In the Norris-monster scene, for instance, a man's head sprouts giant spider's legs and scampers across the floor. In fact, the head is a rubber model. It sits on top of a hidden, radio-controlled toy car. The huge, bald, two-headed dog was also a rubber model. Audiences were both amused and frightened by the new version of *The Thing*. Part of the fun lay in never knowing what the monster would look like next.

Judging from the mess they find, Billy and Kate know that the Gremlins have been here.

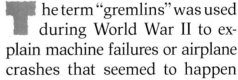

(1984)

# GREMLINS

*color*
*dir* Joe Dante
*pro* Steven Spielberg
*st* Zach Galligan, Phoebe Cates,
    Hoyt Axton
*sp eff* Chris Walas

he term "gremlins" was used during World War II to explain machine failures or airplane crashes that seemed to happen for no good reason. One of the United States' enemies in that war was Japan. Today, Japan sells the U.S. many of its cars and most of its electronic goods. In subtle ways, *Gremlins* plays on modern Americans' fears of being "taken over," not by a foreign country, but by foreign products.

## "With Mogwai Comes Much Responsibility"

Randall Peltzer is an inventor, a dreamer, and a traveling salesman. His latest invention is the "Bathroom Buddy"—a travel kit that spits toothpaste all over him when he tries to demonstrate it.

Traveling salesman Randall Peltzer *(right)* brings his son Billy a cute little Mogwai, which Billy names "Gizmo."

One night, Peltzer tries to sell his Bathroom Buddy to an old, half-blind Chinese man who runs an odd curio shop. While looking around the cluttered shop, Peltzer discovers an old wooden box. Inside is a cute, cuddly, little animal called a Mogwai. Peltzer wants to buy the animal as a present for his teenage son Billy. He offers the shopkeeper $200, but the old man refuses. "With Mogwai," the shopkeeper says, "comes much responsibility."

The shopkeeper's grandson, however, is eager to make the sale. He sneaks the Mogwai out of the shop and delivers it to Peltzer in a dark alley. The boy warns Peltzer that the Mogwai's owner must follow three rules. First, don't expose the Mogwai to strong light, especially sunlight, which will kill it. Second, don't get it wet. And third, never, never, never feed it after midnight. Peltzer says, "Sure, kid," pays for the Mogwai, and heads home to the small town of Kingston Falls.

That night, when Mr. Peltzer returns home from his sales trip, he presents Billy with the box containing the Mogwai. Billy is delighted with the furry brown animal. It has long, pointed ears and big brown eyes. Billy's dad says the Mogwai's name is "Gizmo," and he tells Billy the three rules that must always be followed: no bright lights—especially sunlight—no water, and no food after midnight. Billy plays with Gizmo in his room and even teaches him to sing the notes on his electronic keyboard.

The next night, Billy's friend Pete delivers the Peltzers' Christmas tree. Pete accidentally spills a glass of water on Gizmo, and something incredible happens. Gizmo shakes and screams, his back swells up, and five furry balls pop right out of him. The balls stretch, open up, and turn into five more Mogwais.

The new Mogwais look like Gizmo, but they are not so cuddly. They seem mischievous and rude. One of them spits on the floor. Another one, who has a stripe of white hair on his head, bites young Pete on the finger.

That night, after Billy has gone to bed, he hears his dog Barney howling in pain. He finds him outside, nearly dead, hanging from some Christmas-tree lights. Billy is convinced that the town grouch, Mrs. Deagle, tried to kill Barney, but his dad assures him that the dog was locked inside when the family went to bed. Billy wonders who else might have wanted to kill Barney.

The next day, Billy takes one of the new Mogwais to his high school biology teacher, Mr. Hanson. The teacher is amazed by the little creature, particularly when Billy drops a single drop of water on it and a new Mogwai pops out. Mr. Hanson asks Billy if he may keep one of the Mogwais at school to run some tests.

On the way home, Billy stops by Dorry's Tavern to ask a young woman named Kate for a date. Kate is just closing the saloon when Billy arrives. The last customer to leave, Mr. Futterman, is always complaining about the foreign cars and radios and televisions that people in the United States buy. He tells Billy and Kate that foreigners plant "gremlins" in their machines—little monsters that make things stop working.

That night, Billy is working in his room, trying to ignore his new pets, who are screaming for food. Finally, Billy agrees to feed them, but he first checks the clock to make sure it is not yet midnight. He then feeds the new Mogwais a plate of fried chicken. He offers some chicken to Gizmo, too, but Gizmo is sleepy and just shakes his head. At the same time, down at the high school, Mr. Hanson's Mogwai steals a sandwich and eats it.

The next morning, Billy finds five large, slime-covered pods on his bedroom floor. "Uh oh," says Gizmo. Billy discovers that the Mogwais chewed through the cord on his electric clock. By stopping the clock, they tricked him into feeding them after midnight. Billy rushes to the high school, where the biology teacher is examining his own Mogwai pod. "This is a cocoon," Mr. Hanson says. "Inside he's going through changes. . . . A metamorphosis."

The Mogwais begin to hatch that afternoon, while Billy is working at his job at the bank. Mr. Hanson phones Billy to come right away. When he reaches the darkened classroom, Billy sees Mr. Hanson lying dead on the floor. Billy grabs the phone, but something scratches his hand

Stripe, the meanest Gremlin of all

with a vicious swipe. Whatever it was, it bursts through the wall and disappears.

Billy's mother is cooking in her kitchen when she hears a commotion upstairs. Smoke is pouring out of the pods. Long, ugly claws reach through cracks in the shells. Gizmo hides inside Billy's motorcycle helmet, terrified. The gremlins that emerge from the pods are much bigger than Gizmo, and definitely not cuddly. They have leathery, lizard-like bodies, sharp claws, red eyes, and big bat ears.

Billy calls his mom to warn her what is happening, but the gremlins rip out the telephone wires. Billy's mom is not afraid. She picks up a kitchen knife and goes looking for the creatures. Behind her, their shadows creep along the wall.

Mrs. Peltzer hears a racket coming from the kitchen.

The gremlins are tearing out cupboards and throwing dishes. One of them is licking the inside of a juice machine that Mr. Peltzer invented. Billy's mom reaches out cautiously and switches on the machine. Juiced gremlin flies all over the kitchen.

As the other gremlins bombard her with dishes, Mrs.

Trouble lies ahead for Mrs. Peltzer as she investigates some strange noises coming from upstairs, where the Gremlins are.

Peltzer stabs one and explodes another in the microwave oven. A gremlin hidden in the Christmas tree, however, grabs her from behind. The little monster is ripping Mrs. Peltzer with his claws when Billy rushes in to save his mother. He grabs an antique sword from a wall display and cuts off the gremlin's head.

One gremlin manages to get away. It is "Stripe," the nastiest of the bunch. Billy follows Stripe's footprints through the snow to the YMCA swimming pool. Before Billy can stop him, Stripe leaps into the water. The pool becomes a bubbling green cauldron, and the entire YMCA building fills with smoke and green light. The gremlins are reproducing.

Billy rushes to the sheriff's office, but no one will believe his story. Soon strange things are happening all over town. Thousands of gremlins have invaded Kingston Falls.

The gremlins kill mean old Mrs. Deagle and drive a snowplow through Mr. Futterman's house. All around town, people are being attacked by gremlins. Cars crash, fires are started, people are bitten. Dorry's Tavern has been taken over by gremlins, who are fighting, playing cards, and swinging from ceiling fans. Kate, trapped behind the bar, uses a flash camera to fight her way to the door, blinding the gremlins with bright flashes. At the door, Billy rescues her from a gun-toting gremlin, and together they run to safety.

Billy and Kate hide in the wrecked lobby of the bank building. After a while, the town grows quiet. Billy and Kate slip out of the bank and track the gremlins to a movie theater. Amazingly, the creatures have all gathered in the theater to watch *Snow White and the Seven Dwarfs*. Thousands of the little monsters are happily sitting and singing, "Hi ho, hi ho, it's off to work we go."

In the saloon, the wild Gremlins smoke, drink, dance, play pool
—and arm wrestle.

Billy and Kate open a gas valve in the basement of the theater, start a small fire, then run for their lives. They make it out just before the theater explodes in a huge ball of flame, killing all the gremlins.

All except one, that is. Stripe left the movie early, looking for something to eat at the department store across the street. Billy spots him and goes after him. Inside the department store, Stripe throws saw blades and baseballs at Billy, shoots him with a crossbow, and even tries to kill him with a chain saw. But Gizmo, driving a tiny toy car, comes to Billy's rescue. Just before Stripe can jump into a fountain and multiply again, Gizmo pulls a cord that opens a sunroof. Sunlight streams in and destroys the monster. Luckily, Gizmo's car crashes and he is thrown clear of the deadly light.

That night, the old Chinese man appears at the Peltzers' door to take back his Mogwai. He tells the Peltzers that they are not ready to handle the responsibility of taking care of the Mogwai, but with a kind smile, he turns to Billy and says, "Perhaps someday *you* will be ready."

## "THEY'RE HERE, THEY'RE HERE"

In one scene of *Gremlins*, Billy and Gizmo watch an old movie on television. The movie is *Invasion of the Body Snatchers*, a 1950s film about "seed pods" from outer space. The pods take over people's minds and bodies. Pod-people look just like human beings, but they have no emotions. One of the pod-people tells the film's hero, "Tomorrow you'll be one of us. There's no need for love. Love, desire, ambition, faith—without them life is so simple, believe me." The hero, however, escapes and

**Joe Dante, director of** *Gremlins*

**A scene from** *Invasion of the Body Snatchers*

goes running through the streets shouting "They're here, they're here!"

Americans in the 1950s were worried about losing their unique personalities. People talked about the problem of "conformity," a situation where everyone ends up being like everyone else. *Invasion of the Body Snatchers* played on this fear of conformity, in the same way that *Gremlins* plays on people's fear of things that are too different, too "foreign."

Like monster movies throughout the years, these two films brought people's fears to life. In the end, both movies also left their audiences with a sense of hope. The message of these films is that someday we may be able to triumph over the things that frighten us the most.

# For Further Reading

Aylesworth, Thomas G. *Monsters from the Movies.* Philadelphia: J.B. Lippincott Company, 1972.

Cohen, Daniel. *Horror in the Movies.* New York: Clarion Books, 1982.

———. *Horror Movies.* New York: Gallery Books, 1984.

———. *Masters of Horror.* New York: Clarion Books, 1984.

Edelson, Edward. *Great Monsters of the Movies.* Garden City, N.Y.: Doubleday & Company, 1973.

Everson, William K. *More Classics of the Horror Film.* Secaucus, N.J.: Citadel Press, 1986.

Manchel, Frank. *Terrors of the Screen.* Englewood Cliffs, N.J.: Prentice-Hall, 1970.

# Index